The After

Dellavonte Hune

Anicale Publishing—Madison, WI
ISBN: 978-0-9998967-8-5
Library of Congress Control Number: 2022902603
Title: *The After*
Author: Dellavonte Hune
Digital distribution | 2022
Paperback | 2022

Growing Pains

This collection of poems/ dialogue is a depiction of one's soul. A man obsessed with love, is constantly confronted with harsh reality. This is a written description of his soul as he must go through growing pains. In order to discover who he truly is. There are highs and there are lows; there is ugly and there is beauty. In reality, healing is complicated and here lye the evidence.

Dedication

This page is to honor all the people that has come into my life for the better. Whether it was someone to vent to, a place to crash, a hand to hold, even just believing in me. Some have passed to soon, but their impact lives on to this day. Thank you from the deepest part of my heart.

Tony Robinson
Naton Whitlock
Eric Ranson
Christian Jay Heredia
Savannah Van Horn
Emilio Perez
Trevor Richardet
Justin Noboa
Erica Hune
Nicia Joyner
Angelica Williams
Dj Bell
Rolph Duplan
Alexander Bradburn
Jessica Sawyer

Down That Path

I want to go down that path with you, I want to go to that place most fear going to. Afraid of the endless possibilities they could have. I want to get drunk off the city lights and get high off the country air with you. I want to go down that path with you.

10/02/2010

So, we gone take it back to 8th grade

When I was the skinny kid with the waves

And you were the girl with the smile on her face

So beautiful it could send a rocket out to space

And I was the kid that was clowning for days

And you were the girl stuck in my brain

The Corridors

Dark smokey crowded room
Yet I still feel utterly alone
My soul aches for excitement but only let's in darkness.
A pioneer of self-destruction I breathe in all the bad and hold my
breath until my face turns purple and my vision turns blurry.
I yearn to know what's on the other side
To know what it feels like to let go and to fly. But the chains of
societies expectations hold me grounded.
Oh, how I wish to let my wings spread and reach the corridors of a
new beginning
For now, I watch the starry skyline waiting for my day to arrive.

WORDS

Trails of open promises is where I am lost
Words of great promises hanging off your lips I fall in attempt to
grab a hold of them

You lead me to a place I've never been
Putting faith in my heart of a new beginning

I dove in belief that you were diving with me, but I fall alone and
now I am lost

Lost on my purpose here
I drink to forget
Smoke to ease
Cut to release

The power of words mold and break this world of ours
Choose yours wisely

Flames

Burning ashes of lost memories
Made by someone nonexistent in your life anymore
I feel my skin peel back as I try to recreate you
The burning coal of our memories is what I hold onto
I bathe in flames because forgetting you would be much worse
Call me the man on fire or the man caught in his past

Dandelion

Smothered with memories, I drown in my own doing

Carving your smile out of the skyline I watch it blow freely

Blowing your existence into a dandelion and chasing the remains in
the wind for collateral

Surgeon or thief, you cut deep within me and collect what is yours

Bandits of the night, you chase the brightest star while I follow mine
closely behind

Guardians of our own insecurities, I let you see the skeletons in my
closet

Blue Horizons

I imagine the ocean is the same as someone's soul
Deep blue horizons conceal majestic beauty underneath
Glimpses of life pokes out like dolphins riding the waves

Some attempt to conquer it, but in doing
so, rips out the beauty that makes it, and slaughters your existence
I imagine this is where insecurities were born

The next soul that comes into contact fills the pain the ones before
them had caused
Stirring up the ocean and waves rise and crash down on the
misfortunate

Be the one brave enough to dive headfirst into another soul not to rip
out the beauty beneath the ocean
But to ride with the wave and maybe see things that never poke out
of the surface

Radio Static

Whoever this may reach, I am the misunderstood.

Requesting A Dreamer

I need a dreamer. Someone who will jump from the highest heights in belief that they will fly.
Someone who was told boys wore jeans but decided to wear a squirt because they knew they could be whoever they wanted.

I need a dreamer. Someone who threw away the interchanging personalities, decided to wash off the make-up, and say "fuck you!" To high school expectations.
Someone who cries during happy moments, and laughs through pain
Someone who trips themselves before any bully could, then laughs at them for being too slow.
I need a dreamer. Someone who rejects heartbreak and only let's love in.
Someone who embraces their scars like battle token, a warrior of growth.
Someone who refuses to hide in the shadows of their insecurities.
I need a dreamer. Someone who lives, lives for adventure, love, a story, lives for themselves.
Someone who breaks the shackles that bind them to this world.
A dreamer who climbs those flight of stairs, gets to the top, and jumps in confidence that they will fly.

Notes To You

I can't love myself, so I hope you do.

Oh Fuck

When you lose someone who was your home, and you're like, "oh fuck! I should have had a backup home." Somewhere to fall back on, because now I'm homeless and alone.

Kill Me with Love

If you are about to drown, they say if you take 3 big gulps you'll pass out and drown peacefully. I feel that's ironic, letting in the thing that's trying to kill you and letting it consume you completely. I'm addicted to you. I know you are trying to kill me, but I take 3 big gulps of you and let you consume me. Take my breath away, stop my heart, take away the pain. End my misery.

Anatomy

My occipital lobe only sees you.
My cerebellum is messed up because I only seem balanced when
you're next to me.
My parietal lobe keeps flashing memories of us in my head.
When you touch me, my medulla made my heart race, and shortened
my breathing.
I keep falling because my brain is so caught up with thoughts of you,
that it forgets to tell my pons to send messages to the spinal cord.
My reticular formation is what makes me sweat from my arousal
when you whisper in my ear.
My amygdala is completely shot from all the conflicting emotions I
have about you.

Heartbeat

She is overwhelmed by him. He breathes down her neck, and she can feel her soul escaping her body and going into his. He has her, and he is handling her with so many emotions. He kisses her neck so subtle that it sends chills down her spine. Slowly making his way up to her mouth. But when they're lips connect it's almost like war. His lips ever so tight against hers that a drop of blood falls on her chin.

She watches him as he falls asleep, drawing a line across every inch of his body. He is a sculpture, art to her. The room is silent and at peace when she lays her head on his chest and feel his warmth cover her like a blanket. Then it happens...... bu bump....bu bump. This is when she knows she's in love because the beat of his heart sends tears down her eyes. The slow, steady, calm beat of an inviting heart. What kills her the most is that she imagined that it beat for her. Every beat is him giving a little piece of himself over to her. She doesn't just love him, she's in love with his heart.

She falls asleep with tears in her eyes and a smile on her face. But she wakes up to an empty bed. This is their routine; this is her life. But this time hurt because never had she heard his heart. She never knew she loved him until she felt his heart against her ear whispering sweet nothings to her all night. The worst part of it all is he has her heart, no questions asked. When they are in the middle of it all and her soul lifts from her body into his, it takes her heart with it. She's in love with a man that she barely knows. No, no she's not! She's in love with his heartbeat.

14

Hurting

People cut deep, place their hands inside of you, and rip your heart out. And they get to move on and have normal lives, while you lay in bed every night and wonder why you weren't good enough. For me it's been 4 months, but it doesn't matter if it's been 4 months, 4 days, or 4 years. I'm hurting, your hurting, we're hurting but it's okay. We're allowed to.

In You in Us

I step in the light of the people around me
Sun kissed skin, rejuvenated by the souls of others
Fill my heart with the hopes of your dreams because I cannot
produce my own
Vibrating off the energy you bring
Reborn again in you in us

Deeper

*look deep within the eyes, and at that moment open the corridors of a
Safe Haven and hear angels sing!
What a revolutionary sound, a sound that will make you believe in
any and everything.
Make you believe in love, pain, happiness, make you believe in the
journey in itself*

Thug Harmony

In a position to get it
too gifted to miss it
But I'm sippin on liquids
That's blurring my vision

Straight from the bottle
Pushing on throttle
I'm done with the sorrow
I'll be dead by tomorrow

If I Die

If I were to die today
what would it mean?
what did I provide to this world? what did I truly give?
I hoped that the day I step off this earth people will remember that I
loved wholeheartedly, full throttle, with nothing left in me
I gave everything to love because love is the only thing worth living
for.
And when my time comes just know that I gave it all to a world
without hope; I gave my heart.

I Need You

My very essence clings to your skin
My body wakes up to your every touch
My tongue craves the taste of your lips
I need you
Like lungs need air
Like the body needs the brain
Like the heart needs blood
My soul needs you
When you peel back the flesh,
the muscle and get to the bare bones. They scream to be heard
They scream to feel alive
They scream for you
They need you
I need you

Unconditionally

To be loved unconditionally.
Is to feel scared, anxiety, heartache,
pleasure, confused, lost, sensational,
free, connected, gay, whole.
To feel!

To feel so much it hurts and rises
and spills and trembles across
your skin.

To feel something not tangible
something that can't be caught
by the naked eye
but something you know is real
because you created it together
you nurtured it, fed it, made it stronger
and stronger.

You felt it blossom inside of you
Felt it awaken parts of you, you didn't
even know was asleep.
Creating something inside of you that's
not seen but FELT, unconditionally.

I Miss it

I miss how you thought my awkwardness was charming
Stargazed in the abundance of me
Mesmerized by the rise of my skin, while you trace my outline
I miss the attentiveness in your eyes as I spew my poetry upon your
ears
Craving the taste, a bit more, each time you sink your lips into my
collarbone
I miss the way you thought me struggling to take off my pants before
sex, was sexy
The way your body gasped for air as our bodies are intertwined
I miss the way you made my words steady, my confidence rise, and
my body feel alive

Chances

A chance to say hi
A chance to get to know you
A chance for you to get to know me
A chance to make you smile
A chance to take you out
A chance to make you mine
A chance to show you my demons
A chance for you to accept them
A chance for you
A chance for me

Resurrection

Waves of life seem to crash down, as I hold my breath. Glitters of life fade in the distance, I fall into the darkness. Finally, alone I breath in, taking in all the world's problems in one gulp. I accept my problems as one, and I find peace in the chaos. The glimmer in my eyes fade, as my soul breaks free. I fly under water, rising to the surface. I close my eyes and follow the sound of angels singing. I follow my heart, never once looking back at my lifeless body. Accepting change.

Believe

At that moment I opened them, and I heard angels sing
What a revolutionary sound, a sound that made you believe in
everything
Made you believe in God, because only a higher power could create
such beauty such power
in the most simplistic way possible
Her eyes were from another dimension, and I was so blessed to be
able to open the doorway and to peek inside

Envious

I hear the screams of the stars in the night
Screaming to be heard, screaming not to feel alone
To us they shine bright, but they cannot see their on worth
They do not see their own glow, but only others in the distance
Maybe that's why we connect to the night sky so well
Maybe that's why we reach to the sky, so that we don't feel so alone
anymore
What if they stared at us back?
What if they were envious of our beauty, as we are with theirs

North to South

I cut North to south and split open like a book revealing all my
insecurities
Draining my veins of poison of you
Crying not of physical pain but the pain of you leaving me for good
Forming a new me like clay because of the pieces of you I cut out
I paint a masterpiece of our story with my blood, our last doing. I
make it messing because it seems most fitting
I light a cigarette and watch the rain wash away the last bit of you
and I whisper sorry in hope that the wind catches it and carries it to
your ears.

What if I Told You I loved You?

What if I told you I loved you?
What if I made your stomach flip?
Your heart trip and the Velcro on your lips smile in my direction

What if I cleared the cloudiest of bong bowls?
Down the hardest of liquor
Injected the deadliest of drugs
What if I told I loved you?

Just one more

Just one more kiss
Where your lips refuse to leave mine

Just one more touch
Where your body clings to my skin

Just one more laugh
Where your lungs beg for air

Just one more smile
Where your dimples get deeper

Just one more I love you
Where our troubles fade to the back of your mind and we just exist,
together

Just one more, see you later
Where you're excited for my return because my heart can't take
another goodbye

Call Me What You Want

Call me crazy
Call me ignorant
Call me dangerous
As long as you call me
Call me dumb
Call me annoying
Call me too much
As long as you call me
Call me babe
Call me love
Call me daddy
As long as you call me

Too Much

Sometimes I feel like I am too much.
Maybe I cried too much as a baby, was hungry too much, wanted to be held too much.
So, the world labeled me as needy.
Maybe I smiled too much, opened the door for others too much, gave random compliments too much.
So, the world labeled me as a flirt.
Maybe I danced too much in class, asked too many questions, disagreed too much.
So, the world labeled me as a problem student.
Maybe I loved too much, read too many love stories, had too much passion.
So, the world labeled me as unlovable.
Maybe I wore my pants too low, wore hoodies too much, am out late too much.
So, the world labeled me as a hoodlum
Maybe I'm too much
or
maybe you're too little.

(Signs) Who are They?

Wild and free spirit she is.
Feisty when she speaks her truth.
Independent in all regards.
Excited for whatever tomorrow brings.

Mature in the way he carries himself.
Assertive on everything he wants.
Cardinal sign driving his ambition.
Earthly in practicality and production.

Inconsistent in what she wants.
Reckless in the decisions she make.
Emotionally invested in everything.
Impatient in the process.

Unpredictable in the choices he makes.
Emotions on a constant roller coaster.
Impossible to connect with others.
Stubborn on what he believes in.

Deep intellectual connection to each other.
Pursuing the best versions of one another.
Contrast created their fireworks.
Earth and fire trying to light up their path, together.

Existing

No one ever talks about how hard it is just to exist.
We are force fed ideals, values, and beliefs by the time we first open
our eyes.
There is an unspoken expectation on how our lives are supposed to
go.
But we know, it's more complicated than that.

Some people get showered with love and affection, but still end up on
the needle.
Some people have known nothing but violence but speak words of
poetry as if they were a descend of Shakespeare.
Some people are born alone with no one to guide them, yet they
create this grand family full of support.

It is life that creates our destiny, beautiful chaos.
You can have everything, or you can have nothing, but life makes all
the future endeavors.

But no one stands up and say, we didn't ask for this.
We didn't ask to be born.
We didn't ask to look the way we look.
We didn't ask for pain.
We didn't ask for life, so why do we have to be burdened with all the
chaos it brings?

Ceiling Fan

I've been staring at the ceiling fan lately.
Days turn into nights and tears turn into ash.

Fighting for a voice, yet my words go unheard.
Fighting to be seen, yet my image is unrecognizable.

I've been staring at the ceiling fan lately.
Days turn into weeks and hearts turn into ice.

Fighting for your touch, yet I've already forgotten the feeling.
Fighting for your love, yet I can't remember the last time you said it.

I've been staring at the ceiling fan lately.
Weeks turn into months; life turns into death.

You Win I Win We Lose

You tell me I'm not doing enough
I tell you; you're doing too much
You tell me I overreact
I tell you, you're being dramatic

You start getting petty
I start lashing out
You start going out more
I start keeping to myself

You start seeing me different
I start seeing you change
You start getting distant
I start needing space

You start winning fights
I start winning fights
But we start losing the game

I've Learned

I've learned to bend, stretch, and extend.
Memorizing all the lessons you lend.
Reborn as a new man
How I yearn, to try this love all over again.
The path we walked, was broken and we never knew.
I refused to walk away, so I forged something new.
If you choose to stay, you could walk it too.
You got me on a diet of caffeine and nicotine
Analyzing your steps on what they could mean
I find myself completely lost in a feeling
Whatever step I take, it's going to hurt but I just need a direction
direction
your place keeps becoming my destination
counting sheep to your tempo
banking on your innuendos
I'm lost in the waiting
for your lips to spell my fate
I'm looking for a grand escape
Counting the times, I caught your tears too late
Analyzing every one of our mistakes
Maybe there's a specific time where it all breaks
Maybe I can catch it before you walk away
They say time heals all wounds
So, for now, we wait and wait and wait

For Tonight

Tonight, my skin got goosebumps in remembrance of your touch
Tonight, my mouth started to water because it swore your lips were connected
Tonight, my heart skipped a beep when it saw your picture
Tonight, my body cried and shook because you weren't laying with me
Tonight, I wrote you a letter, but my hand starts to shake before I could finish because it didn't want it to end
Tonight, it's you, it's always been you
So, for tonight I'm yours, and every day after.
In this life, the next life, and everyone after.

Invisible Scars

I have a scar from an absent father
I have a scar from watching a man put his hands on my mother
I have a scar from being called an N word
I have a scar from game days with no family in the stance
I have a scar from when I was told I wasn't black enough to hang
I have a scar from when I was told I was too black to hang
I have a scar from walking down the aisle and seeing more strangers
than family
I have a scar from a friend trying to take my life when I wasn't
looking
I have a scar from a woman telling me she couldn't love me
I have a scar from being told I was too much and another for not
being enough
My scars are invisible but very much real

Last Dance

She asks for this dance, and I happily accept
She takes my hand and I follow
She steps left and I step left
She steps right and I step right
She begins to spin
And I begin to twirl her
She begins to dip
And I begin to catch her
She rises higher and higher
And I hold her up higher and higher
She spins I spin we spin
Again, and again and again
The dance is over, but I can still hear the music. It feels my soul.

Even though she is gone, I can feel her leading the dance.

She stepped left so I step left
She stepped right so I step right
She spun so I begin to twirl her
She dipped so I begin to catch her
She rose and I'm still holding her up
She spun but I never stopped spinning
Again, and again and again

Everywhere

You are everywhere

In every album marked "pretty lady"
In every playlist I ever made, to put you in the mood
In every flashback on Snapchat

You are everywhere

In every good day
In every bad day
In every win
In every loss

You are everywhere

In the pen I write with
In the paper that tells the story
In every poem I've ever written

You are everywhere

In every lonely night
In every dream
In every off day
In every thought

You are everywhere
Yet you are no where

Love Me for Me

I have longed for someone to love me for me
Love my spontaneous outbreaks of dance parties
Love my screeching, belly shaking covers of Adele songs
Love that I need to cuddle, an obsessive amount
Love that our bed full of stuffed animals, isn't up for debate
Love that I get caught in my head for days at a time, because you
know I'm piecing together our future
Love that I take pride in how I look because I am a black man
Love Me for Me
Love that I work harder under pressure
Love that I go to therapy, even though every ounce of me wants to
run
Love that I am an emotional vault, but I open up to you
Love that I fail, but I keep going
Love that I learn, even if it takes longer than others
Love me for me, and all the demons and angels that come with it
Love me for me and I will love you for you
Let's pour into each other and grow

Designed To Love You

I was designed by God herself
To love you
Like circular saws were designed for trees
Like aquariums were designed for fish
Like Ice cream makers were designed for making ice cream
Like computer algorithms were designed for computers
Like dishwashers were designed for dishes
Like a life raft was designed for saving lives
I was designed to love you
In every facet, in everyday, in every life

Don't Bloom

Hearts don't bloom like the use to
Love don't show like it's supposed to
Smiles don't reflect what we've been through

Who?

You've seen me inside and out.
Seen the light and darkness come out.

Watched my tears fall and reach my mouth
Listened to me scream in agony, without making a sound.

Now as time slows down,
And your presence fades out.
who's going to love me now?

All the fights in rage,
I've seen your words fade out

All those attempts to be seen,
I finally catch a glimpse on your way out.

Now as time slows down,
And you're laying down.
Who gets to hold you now?

Drug House

*Needles spread across the table, as souls are scattered across the
room floor.
Dry death stench air is all I smell, and cries of an end is all I hear.*

*Needles read, acceptance, chance, love, commitment, and hope.
Souls of the chosen to call out to me, to join them in the darkness,
their new light*

*I choose love to be my fatal flaw, as I inject my veins and fill myself
with poison.
Eyes spinning back as my soul peels off its external skin, free of its
superficial prison of judgement.
My soul lays with the others, free of discernment and welcomed with
acceptance.*

*We fill ourselves with things we were not given in the developmental
stage of our lives, and we let it kill us slow, like a drug.*

Prosper

May the sun radiate your skin.
May you heal from your trauma.
May you prosper.

May you break free of the shackles that hold you down.
May your mind find the answers that you are seeking.
May you prosper.

May you find love again
May it be stronger than before
May you be stronger than you once were.

May you prosper

Inhale Exhale

Inhale exhale, you know that you are scared
Inhale exhale, you know that you are aware
Inhale exhale, you know that it's not fair

Inhale exhale, I will always be right there
Inhale exhale, I will always be your bear
Inhale exhale, I will always move with care

Inhale exhale, we are soaring through the air
Inhale exhale, we are unique, distinct, rare
Inhale exhale, we are determined to get there

Healing

Sometimes healing is lying in bed, not showering for days.
Sometimes healing is running the streets with your friends, living
young and wild!
Sometimes healing is shaking and crying uncontrollably until you
pass out.
Sometimes healing is spending time with your family because you
don't want to be alone.
Sometimes healing is staring down a barrel for hours.
Sometimes healing feels good and sometimes it doesn't.
But we must feel to heal, so feel it all and when you're ready... Heal.

Thank You

Thank you for loving me

Thank you for the laughs
Thank you for the cries
Thank you for the nights in your arms

Thank you for the lessons
Thank you for the blessings
Thank you for the words of affection

Thank you for the memories
Thank you for the pleasantries
Thank you for loving the bad days as much as the good ones.

Thank you for showing me how to love myself

Get You

Get who? Get you.
You be in your own mind; nobody can stress you.
Living young, driving fast, I pray nobody test you.

Get who? Get you.
The pain is in the past, don't have to worry about what's next boo.
You be in the lights, so nobody going to neglect you.

Get who? Get you.
Your light is of abundance, so when you pop out it spread too.
You too far in advance, so nobody going to get near you.

Get who? Get you?? I think not.

Twisted Fantasy

I secretly crave the darkness.
The feeling of cutting through the shell of our mortality, is so
liberating.
Peeling back the bull shit and seeing your true form.
Watching your soul breathing reluctant breathes.
Who works when your soul needs a break?
Lathered in tar from all the broken promises, your body thought was
truth.
Smothered in hypercritical advice from other miserable souls.

Trying to find meaning in this twisted fantasy.

Brown Skin

I drink from the fountain
My youth is so resounding
I guess it's that brown skin

Chocolate dream has your heart pounding
Imagining how I would look going down in
Must be that brown skin

My skin starts glowing when that sun rising
Want me to outline every inch of your horizon
Has to be that brown skin

Time Traveler

Oh dear, how your lips reflect god's gift.
How your eyes melt the coldest flakes.
How your smile lifts a room and defy gravity.
How your touch, plucks at my heart strings.

Oh dear, how I've seen those lips cry out in agony.
How those eyes send showers to our bedroom.
How your smile bent at the edges, rusted from damage.
How your touch grew more distance, until non-existent.

Oh dear, how I've seen it all.
Seen us reach the highest heights,
Only to fall.
I'm a time traveler you see.
No longer connected, so I live through the memories.

From The Bottom Up

My beautiful flower child

You were born to be free.
Glistening in the sun light.
Beautiful and bright, as I expected.
Yet, you still bloomed!

I had growing to do myself.
I didn't always get it right.
I nurtured your growth, and growing pains.

I planted you and watered you regularly.
I brought you home with me.
I found your seed on a trail one day.

You Can't Touch Me

I walk on clouds and watch the rain fall.
Been watching the phone, but you ain't call.
Found a tree with a bunch of love and I ate them all.

We consume love, envy, and jealously.
We apply them to the skin, like a remedy.
Poison our minds with ideas of what we could be.

We put ourselves on clouds, not to be seen.
Only letting the three pillars get in between.
Yet, the message is still clearer than a vivid dream.

You can't touch me.

Here But Gone

Can you miss the lips that bless yours as soon as they part?
Can you miss the road trips, where we are singing at the top of our
lungs as we pull into the driveway?
Can you miss the sound of someone sleeping as you watching them
fade into another world?
Can you miss the life you built before you say your goodbyes?
Can you miss something that was never really yours in the first
place, no matter how much you prayed it would be one day?
Can you miss something that has not left you yet, but you know that
it will?

No Saving

The days bleed through the sun
The nights bleed through the moon
The time bleeds through the clock
Yet, there's no saving

Your touch bleeds through my skin
Your voice bleeds through my ears
Your words bleed through my heart
Yet, there's no saving

Courage bleeds through my pride
Hope bleeds through my mind
Love bleeds through my soul
Yet, there's no saving

Gods Not Finished

I know that her hands really in it.
Smoothing out the bumps,
Don't need no dents with it

I know the plot line seems endless.
Even though the screen dark,
Just know there still be an image

The good times, the bad times,
And what all comes with it.
Stretch out your hands,
And ask for forgiveness.

Cause God not finished.

Diamond

Will I crack or form like a diamond?
Can't express the immense pressure, that I'm in.
I feel the dirt compacting, buried alive, I feel confined in.
In my own mind, I scream and cry because of the sirens.
On a journey I saw the quicksand, and I dived in.
Going deeper and deeper, I find comfort in the silence.
This is my journey, those are my demons, there's no more relying.
This is my pressure, this is my truth, I am a diamond.

I Still Do

In the shower or in the rain
In the ovens heat or hell's flame
In the deepest seas or in the trees
I still do

Where the birds fly, and the angels sing
Where the people dance in deep romance
Where the love is love and plenty around
I still do

When the rain is endless, and the clouds are grey
When the clocks have arthritis and time is slow
When the passion is fading, and you must go
Just know, I still do

Final Message

If you touch the flower, she might bite you back.
Love can be just as intense, as a heart attack.
Promises are nothing if there's no truth attached.

Time is gone, but the images make it hard to detach.
Words are final, there's no taking them back.
Yet the heart will still beat, and there is peace in that.

The journey will suck, there's no denying that.
The pain will seem endless, but you mustn't retract.
Go find your happiness, there's no time to take steps back.

About the Author

Dellavonte Hune is a Madison local. Born at St. Mary's hospital, and raised in Sun Prairie. He graduated from Sun Prairie High in 2015 and went to play collegiate lacrosse at Benedictine University for a year. In 2017 he decided to join the Marine Corps, which he served for 4 years Honorably. He was deployed in 2018-2019 to Romania, Jordan, Kuwait, Dubai, Latvia, and Germany. He officially left active duty in February 2021, and moved back to Wisconsin to reunite with his family. Now that he's back, he has done a tremendous amount of reflection, and has written a book of poetry about his healing process.

CPSIA information can be obtained
at www.ICGtesting.com
Printed in the USA
LVHW092157170322
713764LV00017B/232

9 780999 896785